Activity Book

MOTION, FORCES, AND ENERGY

Prentice Hall
Englewood Cliffs, New Jersey
Needham, Massachusetts

Activity Book

PRENTICE HALL SCIENCE
Motion, Forces, and Energy

ISBN 0-13-987900-5

  3 4 5 6 7 8 9 10   96 95 94 93

Prentice Hall
A Division of Simon & Schuster
Englewood Cliffs, New Jersey 07632

Contents

To the Teacher

The materials in the *Activity Book* are designed to assist you in teaching the *Prentice Hall Science* program. These materials will be especially helpful to you in accommodating a wide range of student ability levels. In particular, the activities have been designed to reinforce and extend a variety of science skills and to encourage critical thinking, problem solving, and discovery learning. The highly visual format of many activities heightens student interest and enthusiasm.

All the materials in the *Activity Book* have been developed to facilitate student comprehension of, and interest in, science. Pages intended for student use may be made into overhead transparencies and masters or used as photocopy originals. The reproducible format allows you to have these items easily available in the quantity you need. All appropriate answers to questions and activities are found at the end of each section in a convenient Answer Key.

CHAPTER MATERIALS

In order to stimulate and increase student interest, the *Activity Book* includes a wide variety of activities and worksheets. All the activities and worksheets are correlated to individual chapters in the student textbook.

Table of Contents

Each set of chapter materials begins with a Table of Contents that lists every component for the chapter and the page number on which it begins. The Table of Contents also lists the number of the page on which the Answer Key for the chapter activities and worksheets begins. In addition, the Table of Contents page for each chapter has a shaded bar running along the edge of the page. This shading will enable you to easily spot where a new set of chapter materials begins.

Whenever an activity might be considered a problem-solving or discovery-learning activity, it is so marked on the Contents page. In addition, each activity that can be used for cooperative-learning groups has an asterisk beside it on the Contents page.

First in the chapter materials is a Chapter Discovery. The Chapter Discovery is best used prior to students reading the chapter. It will enable students to discover for themselves some of the scientific concepts discussed within the chapter. Because of their highly visual design, simplicity, and hands-on approach to discovery learning, the Discovery Activities are particularly appropriate for ESL students in a cooperative-learning setting.

Chapter Activities

Chapter activities are especially visual, often asking students to draw conclusions from diagrams, graphs, tables, and other forms of data. Many chapter activities enable the student to employ problem-solving and critical-thinking skills. Others allow the student to utilize a discovery-learning approach to the topics covered in the chapter. In addition, most chapter activities are appropriate for cooperative-learning groups.

Laboratory Investigation Worksheet

Each chapter of the textbook contains a full-page Laboratory Investigation. A Laboratory Investigation worksheet in each set of chapter materials repeats the textbook Laboratory Investigation and provides formatted space for writing observations and conclusions. Students are aided by a formatted worksheet, and teachers can easily evaluate and grade students' results and progress. Answers to the Laboratory Investigation are provided in the Answer Key following the chapter materials, as well as in the Annotated Teacher's Edition of the textbook.

Answer Key

At the end of each set of chapter materials is an Answer Key for all activities and worksheets in the chapter.

SCIENCE READING SKILLS

Each textbook in *Prentice Hall Science* ends with a special feature called the Science Gazette. Each gazette contains three articles.

The first article in every Science Gazette—called Adventures in Science— describes a particular discovery, innovation, or field of research of a scientist or group of scientists. Some of the scientists profiled in Adventures in Science are well known; others are not yet famous but have made significant contributions to the world of science. These articles provide students with firsthand knowledge about how scientists work and think, and give some insight into the scientists' personal lives as well.

Issues in Science is the second article in every gazette. This article provides a nonbiased description of a specific area of science in which various members of the scientific community or the population at large hold diverging opinions. Issues in Science articles introduce students to some of the "controversies" raging in science at the present time. While many of these issues are debated strictly in scientific terms, others involve social issues that pertain to science as well.

The third article in every Science Gazette is called Futures in Science. The setting of each Futures in Science article is some 15 to 150 years in the future and describes some of the advances people may encounter as science progresses through the years. However, these articles cannot be considered "science fiction," as they are all extrapolations of current scientific research.

The Science Gazette articles can be powerful motivators in developing an interest in science. However, they have been written with a second purpose in mind. These articles can be used as science readers. As such, they will both reinforce and enrich your students' ability to read scientific material. In order to better assess the science reading skills of your students, this *Activity Book* contains a variety of science reading activities based on the gazette articles. Each gazette article has an activity that can be distributed to students in order to evaluate their science reading skills.

There are a variety of science reading skills included in this *Activity Book*. These skills include Finding the Main Idea, Previewing, Critical Reading, Making Predictions, Outlining, Using Context Clues, and Making Inferences. These basic study skills are essential in understanding the content of all subject matter, and they can be particularly useful in the comprehension of science materials. Mastering such study skills can help students to study, learn new vocabulary terms, and understand information found in their textbooks.

Contents

*Appropriate for cooperative learning

Chapter Discovery
What Is Motion?

A Walk in the Park

Background Information

Although you may never have given much thought to your activity the last time you walked from one place to another, you were actually obeying important physical laws. You exhibited motion. Motion is movement from one place to another in a certain amount of time. In this activity you will take measurements to describe your motion and determine a relationship that can be used to describe motion.

Materials
stopwatch
meterstick
masking tape

Procedure
Part A
1. Place a small piece of masking tape on the floor or ground in an open area where you can walk freely.

2. Use a meterstick to measure 5 m from the tape. Mark this spot with another small piece of masking tape.

3. Hold the stopwatch and stand at either piece of tape. Start the stopwatch as you begin to walk at a normal pace in a straight line toward the other mark.

4. Stop the stopwatch when you reach the mark. Record the time it took you to walk 5 m.

5. Repeat steps 3 and 4 walking more rapidly than your normal pace. Record your time.

6. Repeat steps 3 and 4 walking more slowly than your normal pace. Record your time.

Part B
1. Leave only one piece of tape in place. Stand on that mark, holding the other piece of tape and the stopwatch.

2. Start the stopwatch and begin walking. Stop walking after 5 sec.

3. Mark the spot where you stopped with the tape. Use the meterstick to measure the distance you walked. Record your measurement.

4. Repeat steps 2 and 3 walking more rapidly than your normal pace.

5. Repeat steps 2 and 3 walking more slowly than your normal pace.

Observations
Part A

Data Table

	Distance (m)	Time (sec)
Trial 1	5	
Trial 2	5	
Trial 3	5	

Part B

Data Table

	Distance (m)	Time (sec)
Trial 1		5
Trial 2		5
Trial 3		5

Analysis and Conclusions

1. Was your time the same for each of the trials in Part A? If not, why do you think the times varied?

   _____

   _____

   _____

   _____

2. How would all of the times have changed if the distance between the two marks were increased? Decreased?

   _____

   _____

   _____

   _____

3. Was the distance you walked the same in each of the trials in Part B? If not, why did it vary?

_____

_____

_____

_____

4. How would the distance walked change if the length of time you measured were increased? Decreased?

_____

_____

_____

_____

5. Describe a relationship between the distance you walk, the time it takes you to walk, and how fast or slow you walk.

_____

_____

_____

_____

Activity

What Is Motion?

A Speedy Journey

Use the graph below to answer the questions about the journeys of two cars.

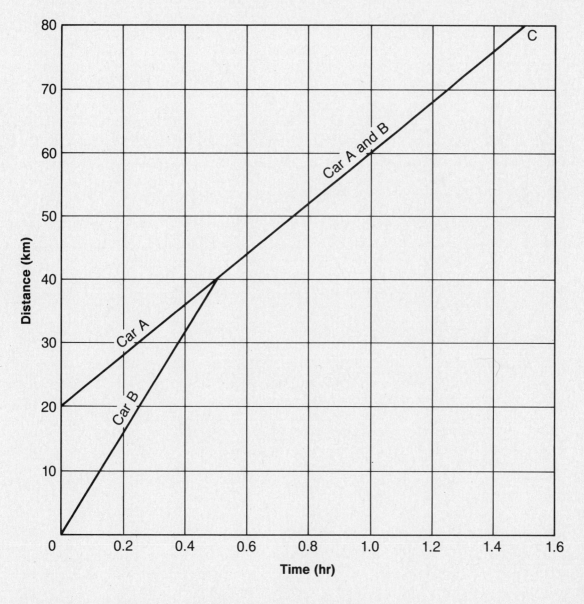

1. How far did car A travel before it met car B? _____

2. How long had the two cars been traveling before they met? _____

3. How far did both cars travel at the same speed? _____

4. How long did it take both cars to get to point C? _____

5. Which car had constant speed? _____ ? What was its

speed? _____

6. What were the speeds of the other car? _____ _____

Activity

Amusement Park Physics

Think about the motion taking place in an amusement park. Consider several rides, such as the roller coaster, Ferris wheel, derby cars, log flume, spinning rides, bumper cars, and any others you can think of.

1. Which rides have constant speed?

_____

_____

_____

2. Which rides have circular motion?

_____

_____

_____

3. Which rides accelerate?

_____

_____

_____

4. Explain how you reached your conclusions for each question.

_____

_____

_____

_____

5. Design a ride that you would like to see in an amusement park. Include the characteristics of motion it would involve.

_____

_____

_____

_____

Calculations of Motion

Solve the following problems. Show all your work. Remember to include the correct units.

1. A jogger runs the first 1000 m of a race in 250 sec. What is the jogger's speed?

2. A Space Shuttle travels in orbit at 21,000 km/hr. How far will it travel after 5 hr?

Problems 3 and 4 refer to the table, which summarizes Jack's ride on his new skateboard.

Time (sec)	Distance (m)
0	0
5	30
10	70
15	90
20	120

3. What was Jack's speed from T = 5 sec to T = 10 sec?

4. What was Jack's average speed for the entire ride?

5. A car accelerates from 0 to 72 km/hour in 8 sec. What is the car's acceleration?

6. A science student drops a rock down a mine shaft. If it takes 3 sec for the rock to hit the bottom of the shaft, what is the speed of the rock just before impact?

7. A space ship is traveling at 20,000 m/sec. At T = 5 sec, the rocket thrusters are turned on. At T = 55 sec, the space ship reaches a speed of 24,000 m/sec. What is the space ship's acceleration?

Activity

Speed, Velocity, and Acceleration

Use the following terms to identify the motion represented in each graph or diagram.

constant speed
average speed
velocities in the same direction

acceleration
deceleration
velocities in opposite directions

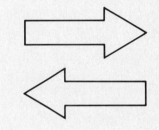

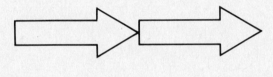

1. _____

3. _____

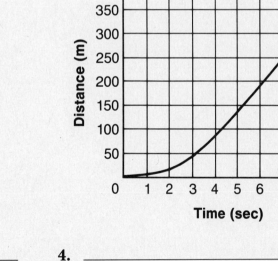

2. _____

4. _____

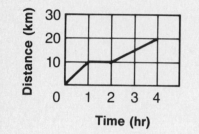

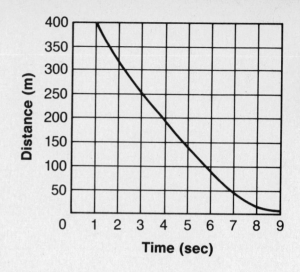

5. _____

6. _____

Activity

Working With Examples of Motion

Solve the following problems. Show all your work. Remember to include the correct units.

1. A student practicing for a track meet ran 250 m in 30 sec.

   a. What was her average speed?

   b. If on the following day she ran 300 m in 30 sec, by how much did her speed increase?

2. A car traveled 1025 km from El Paso to Dallas in 13.5 hr. What was its average velocity?

3. How fast was a plane flying if it traveled 400 km in 30 min?

4. A student walks 10 blocks to a computer store. (Assume all the blocks are equal length.)

   a. How long will it take him to reach the computer store if he walks 3 blocks in 2 min?

   b. What is his average velocity?

5. If the average speed of a car is 45 km/hr, how far can it travel in 40 min?

6. The speed of light is 3×10^8 m/sec. How long does it take light to travel the 149×10^9 m distance from the sun to the Earth?

7. A driver starts his parked car and within 5 sec reaches a velocity of 54 km/hr as he travels east. What is his acceleration?

8. Falling objects drop with an average acceleration of 9.8 m/sec/sec, or 9.8 m/sec^2. If an object falls from a tall building, how long will it take before it reaches a speed of 49 m/sec?

9. A car traveling north with a velocity of 30 m/sec slows down to a velocity of 10 m/sec within 10 sec. What is the car's deceleration?

10. A steel ball whose mass is 100 g is rolling at a rate of 2.8 m/sec. What is its momentum?

11. A marble is rolling at a velocity 100 cm/sec with a momentum of 10,000 g-cm/sec. What is its mass?

12. An object whose mass is 3 kg is fired from a cannon, giving it a forward momentum of 1050 kg-m/sec. What is its velocity?

_____ *Laboratory Investigation* _____

Measuring Constant Speed

Problem
What is the shape of a distance–time graph of constant speed?

Materials *(per student)*
pencil
graph paper
metric ruler

Procedure
1. The illustration on this page represents a series of flash shots taken of a dry-ice puck sliding across the floor. The time between each flash is 0.1 second. Study the illustration carefully.

2. Copy the sample data table on a sheet of graph paper.

3. Position the 0-cm mark of the metric ruler on the front edge of the first puck. This position will represent distance 0.0 cm at time 0.0 second. Record these data in your data table.

4. Without moving the ruler, determine the distance of each puck from the first one.

5. Record each distance to the nearest 0.1 cm in your data table.

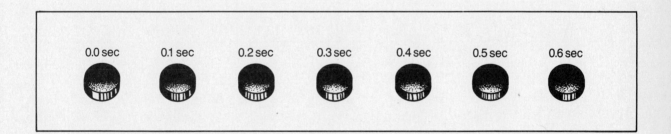

0.0 sec   0.1 sec   0.2 sec   0.3 sec   0.4 sec   0.5 sec   0.6 sec

Observations

Time (sec)	Distance (cm)
0.0	0.0
0.1	
0.2	
0.3	
0.4	
0.5	
0.6	

Make a distance–time graph using the data in your table. Plot the distance on the vertical, or Y, axis and the time on the horizontal, or X, axis.

Analysis and Conclusions

1. What is the shape of the graph? _____

_____

2. Is the speed constant? Explain. _____

_____

3. Calculate the average speed. _____

_____

4. How will the graph change with time? _____

_____

5. **On Your Own**   Suppose you are ice skating around a rink at a constant speed. Then you get tired so you stop moving your feet and glide along the ice. How would your distance–time graph look?

_____

_____

Answer Key

Chapter Discovery: A Walk in the Park

1. Students should show shortest time for trial 2 and longest time for trial 3. Students should realize that they walked at different rates. 2. All of the times would increase if the length was increased and decrease if the length was decreased. 3. Students should show the greatest distance in trial 2 and the shortest distance in trial 3. Students should realize that walking faster enables them to walk a greater distance in the same amount of time. 4. The distance would increase if the time was increased and decrease if the time was decreased. 5. The faster you walk and the more time you have, the greater distance you will move.

Activity: A Speedy Journey

1. 40 km   2. 0.5 hr or 30 min   3. 40 km
4. 1.5 hr or 90 min   5. A; 60 km/hr
6. 80 km/hr; 60 km/hr

Discovery Activity: Amusement Park Physics

Answers will vary depending on students' experiences. Check descriptions to see that answers are logical.

Problem-Solving Activity: Working With Examples of Motion

1a. 8.3 m/sec   b. 1.7 m/sec   2. 75.9 km/hr   3. 13.3 km/min   4a. 6.7 min
b. 1.5 blocks/min   5. 30 km   6. 8.28 min

or 497 sec   7. 3 m/sec/sec, east   8. 5 sec
9. 2m/sec/sec   10. 280 g-m/sec   11. 100 g
12. 350 m/sec

Problem-Solving Activity: Calculations of Motion

1. 4 m/sec   2. 105,000 km   3. 1.5 hr
4. 8 m/sec   5. 6 m/sec   6. 9 km/hr/sec
7. 2 m/sec/sec   8. 29.4 m/sec   9. 2.04 sec
10. 80 m/sec/sec

Activity: Speed, Velocity, and Acceleration

1. velocities in the same direction
2. constant speed   3. velocities in opposite directions   4. acceleration   5. average speed
6. deceleration

Laboratory Investigation Worksheet: Measuring Constant Speed

Observations Students' data table should show that distance increases constantly by about 2.1 cm for each time interval.
Analysis and Conclusions   1. Straight line.
2. Yes. The graph of time vs. distance for constant speed is a straight line.
3. 21.8 cm/sec.   4. It will continue along the same straight line.   5. Once you slowed up, the slope of the graph would decrease steadily until you stopped, when it would become a horizontal segment.

Contents

*Appropriate for cooperative learning

Name _____ Class _____ Date _____

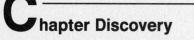 **hapter Discovery**   **The Nature of Forces**

CHAPTER
2

Table Hockey

You may be familiar with a tabletop game in which a flat disk floats on small jets of air as it is hit back and forth by two players. In this activity you play a similar form of tabletop hockey involving coins.

To begin, obtain several different coins. Put your finger on a quarter and hit it into a stationary dime.

1. What happens to the dime?

_____

_____

Hit the dime again. Observe how far it travels. Try hitting it softly and observe how far it travels. Then hit it harder. Again observe how far it travels.

2. How is the distance traveled by the dime affected by how hard you hit it?

_____

_____

3. Describe some sports, games, or examples that show the relationship between how far something moves and how hard you push or throw it.

_____

_____

_____

Now try hitting into different coins. First try a penny, then a quarter, and then tape several coins together. The larger or heavier the combination of coins, the more massive it is.

4. Compare the motion of these coins with that of the dime. How are they different? How are they alike?

_____

_____

_____

© Prentice-Hall, Inc.

5. Describe examples you encounter in which the more massive an object is, the more difficult it is to move.

_____

_____

_____

Gather your coins together again. Take a dime and hit it into another dime. But this time, let go of the coin before it hits the other coin.

6. What happens to the coins after they collide?

_____

_____

Repeat this step with various coins, from least massive to most massive.

7. What happens to the motion of the coins as mass increases?

_____

_____

_____

8. Realizing that objects do not tend to move on their own, what can you say about the motion of the coins?

_____

_____

_____

9. What relationship can you state about the force with which something is hit and its motion?

_____

_____

_____

10. With this activity in mind, can you explain why a batter takes a large swing to knock a ball over the fence?

_____

_____

_____

Activity

To the Finish Line

The force applied by contestants A, B, and C is equal. The masses of the objects they are pushing are indicated. Based on this information, answer the following questions.

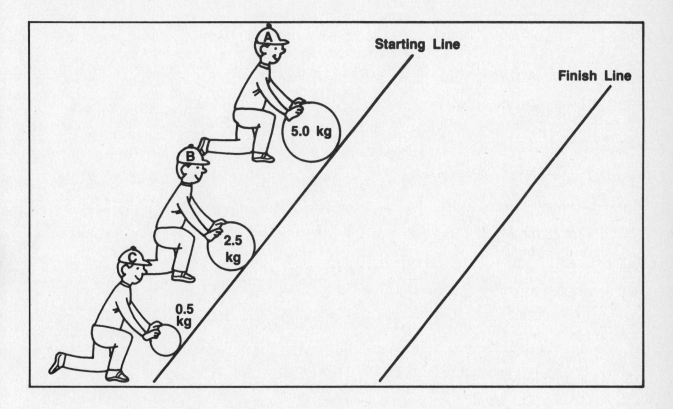

1. The contestant whose object accelerates most is _____ .

2. The contestant whose object accelerates less than B's is _____ .

3. The contestant whose object accelerates twice as much as A's is _____ .

4. The contestant whose object accelerates ten times less than C's is _____ .

5. Assuming a force of 50 N is applied to each object by each contestant, what is the

   acceleration of object A? _____ B? _____ C? _____

6. Now suppose the race ends in a tie and all objects have the same acceleration. This means that the force applied to each object is different. If the acceleration is

   50 m/sec, what force is applied by A? _____ By B? _____ By C? _____

Working With Forces

Solve the following problems. Show all your work. Remember to include the correct units.

1. What is the force on a 1-kg ball that is falling freely due to the pull of gravity? (Neglect air resistance.)

2. A man has a mass of 66 kg on the Earth. What is his weight?

3. A girl on roller skates accelerates at a rate of 2 m/sec/sec with a force of 100 N. What is her mass?

4. A person weighs 540 N on the Earth. What is the person's mass? What would the person weigh on the moon where the acceleration due to gravity is 1.67 N/kg?

5. An elevator has a mass of 1000 kg.
   a. What is the tension force on its cables when it is stationary?

   b. What force is needed to accelerate it upward at a rate of 2 m/sec/sec?

   c. What force is needed to accelerate it downward at a rate of 2 m/sec/sec?

6. An originally stationary car with a mass of 1500 kg reaches a velocity of 15 m/sec 5 sec after starting. What is the car's acceleration? How much force was required to reach this acceleration?

7. An astronaut has a mass of 50 kg.

   a. How much does she weigh before liftoff?

   b. When her space vehicle is 6400 km above the Earth's surface, she will weigh one quarter of what she weighed on the Earth.

      (1) What does she weigh at that point in space?

      (2) What is the acceleration on her mass at that point in space?

8. A 7000-kg plane is launched from an aircraft carrier in 2 sec by a force of 350,000 N. What is the plane's acceleration? What is the plane's velocity?

Activity

Newton's First Law of Motion

Newton's first law of motion states that an object in motion will continue to move at constant speed in a straight line. Only an outside force can change the speed or direction. If the object is at rest, it will remain at rest, unless an outside force is exerted on it.

Suppose you are standing in the aisle of a jumbo jet parked at its terminal. You jump straight up. Where will you land? That is an easy question to answer. You will land in the same place from which you jumped. But now suppose the jet is moving at a speed of 600 km/hr. You jump straight up again. Where will you land? Try this activity and see if you can answer the question correctly.

1. While standing still, throw a small rubber ball straight up about 2 or 3 m high. Does it land in your hand?

   _____

2. Now walk at a constant speed and throw the ball straight up. Where does the ball land?

   _____

3. Continue walking at a constant speed. This time, stop instantly just after you release the ball upward. Where does the ball land?

   _____

4. Continue walking at a constant speed. Just after you release the ball upward, break into a run. Where does the ball land?

   _____

5. Continue walking at a constant speed. Just after you release the ball upward, make a sharp right turn. Where does the ball land?

   _____

6. Where would you land on the jumbo jet that is moving at 600 km/hr?

   _____

Newton's Third Law of Motion

Newton's third law states that for every action there is an equal and opposite reaction. For every force exerted, there must be an equal and opposite force. A single force cannot exist! If a ball bounces off a wall, the wall moves in the opposite direction of the rebounding ball. Of course, the wall is attached to the Earth and the movement is very small. But what if the wall could move? Could this principle be used to move a cart? Try this activity and see.

Use the following materials to make your rolling backboard: two wooden boards, one board at least 10 cm in width, a hammer, nails, a super-bounce ball or tennis ball, two thumbtacks, a length of string, and a skateboard or other set of wheels.

Now follow the steps listed below and see Newton's third law of motion in action-reaction!

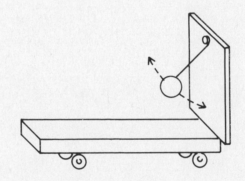

1. Nail the two boards together to form the letter "L."

2. Mount the narrower board on a set of wheels. Use the accompanying figure to help you with your construction.

3. Using thumbtacks, attach a piece of string to the top of the backboard and to the ball.

4. Pull the ball away from the backboard. Let it go. When the ball bounces off the backboard, what should happen to the cart?

_____

_____

_____

5. Let the ball bounce off the backboard several times.

6. Did the cart continue to move forward? Can you explain what happened?

_____

_____

_____

_____

_____

_____

ctivity

Motion Mathematics

1. How long would it take a car to return to its starting place if it traveled 180 km at an average speed of 90 km/hr and returned to its starting place along the same straightline path? (Neglect the time that the car takes to turn around.)

2. If a moving object travels north for a distance of 100 m in 20 sec, what is its velocity?

3. A car traveling south at a velocity of 30 m/sec slows down to a velocity of 10 m/sec in 10 sec. Calculate the deceleration.

4. What force would be required to accelerate a 40-kg mass by 4 m/sec/sec?

5. How large is a mass if a force of 100 N is required to accelerate it by 1 m/sec/sec?

6. Two metal spheres are the same size but have different masses. They are dropped simultaneously from a cliff. Compare their accelerations at midpoint in their fall. Explain your answer.

7. Does one mass reach the midpoint before the other? Explain your answer.

8. If weight is the product of mass times the acceleration on mass due to gravity, what is the mass of a person who weighs 500 N? (The acceleration due to gravity is 9.8 m/sec/sec.)

9. What acceleration can a 1-N force give to a 1-kg object?

10. A tow truck is towing a car. If the tow truck stops abruptly and the car collides with it, what is the relation between the forces on both vehicles?

_____ *Laboratory Investigation* _____

Will an Elephant Fall Faster Than a Mouse?

Problem
Does mass affect the rate of fall?

Materials *(per group)*
wood block, 10 cm × 15 cm × 2.5 cm
Styrofoam pad, 10 cm × 15 cm × 2.5 cm
sheet of notebook paper
triple-beam balance

Procedure
1. Use the triple-beam balance to determine the masses of the block, Styrofoam pad, and paper. Record each mass to the nearest 0.1 gram.

2. Hold the block and foam pad horizontally at arm's length. The largest surface area of each object should be parallel to the ground.

3. Release both the block and the foam pad at the same time. Observe if they land at the same time or if one hits the ground before the other.

4. Repeat step 3 several times. Record your results.

5. Repeat steps 2 to 4 for the foam pad and the paper.

6. Crumple the paper into a tight ball.

7. Compare the falling rates of the crumpled paper and the foam pad. Record your observations.

8. Compare the falling rates of the crumpled paper and the wood block. Record your observations.

Observations

Object	Mass	Falling Rate (comparative)
Wood block		
Styrofoam pad		
Paper (uncrumpled)		
Paper (crumpled)		

1. Which reaches the ground first, the wood block or the foam pad? _____
_____

2. Are your results the same in each trial? _____
_____

3. Which reaches the ground first, the foam pad or the uncrumpled paper? _____
_____

4. Which reaches the ground first, the foam pad or the crumpled paper? _____
_____

Analysis and Conclusions
1. Galileo stated that two bodies with different masses fall at the same rate. Do your observations verify his hypothesis? Explain your answer.
_____
_____

2. Did crumpling the paper have any effect on its falling rate? Explain your answer.
_____
_____

3. Now answer this question: Would an elephant fall faster than a mouse? Explain your answer.
_____
_____

4. On Your Own Design and perform an experiment that compares different objects made out of the same material.
_____
_____

Answer Key

Chapter Discovery: Table Hockey

1. When hit by the quarter, the dime travels a certain distance.   **2.** The harder you hit the dime, the farther it travels.   **3.** Answers will vary. Some examples may be shooting a basketball, throwing a baseball, throwing darts, playing skeeball, or pushing a grocery cart.   **4.** Like the dime, these combinations of coins move when hit. But the more massive the combination, the harder you must hit it to make it move the same distance.   **5.** Answers will vary. Some examples are lifting a heavy grocery bag versus a light one, a large bag of garbage instead of a small one, or a heavy book bag instead of a light one.   **6.** The first dime stops and the other moves.   **7.** As mass increases, the coin moves a smaller distance with the same force.   **8.** The coins had to be pushed in order to move.   **9.** The harder something is hit, the farther and faster it moves.   **10.** The baseball player needs a large force to hit the ball a great distance. If not, the ball would only reach the infield.

Activity: To the Finish Line

1. C **2.** A **3.** B **4.** A **5.** A: 100 m/sec/sec B: 20 m/sec/sec C: 10 m/sec/sec **6.** A: 25 N B: 125 N C: 250 N

Problem-Solving Activity: Working With Forces

1. 9.8 N **2.** 650 N **3.** 50 kg **4a.** 55.1 kg **b.** 92 N **5a.** 9800 N **b.** 2000 N upward **c.** 2000 N downward **6a.** 3m/sec/sec **b.** 4500 N **7a.** 490 N **b.** 122.5 N, 2.45 m/sec/sec **8a.** 50 m/sec/sec **b.** 100 m/sec

Discovery Activity: Newton's First Law of Motion

1. Yes.   **2.** The ball lands in your hand.   **3.** The ball lands in front of you.   **4.** It lands behind you.   **5.** It lands behind and to the left of you, assuming a 90° turn.   **6.** You would land in the same spot from which you jumped.

Discovery Activity: Newton's Third Law of Motion

4. The cart should move forward.   **6.** Answers will vary. They should include the observation that the cart keeps moving forward each time the ball bounces off the backboard. This is action-reaction, or Newton's third law of motion. Because the backboard is on wheels, its reaction movement can be seen.

Problem-Solving Activity: Motion Mathematics

1. 4 hours   **2.** 5 m/sec   **3.** 2 m/sec/sec **4.** 160 N   **5.** 100 kg   **6.** Since gravity is the force that causes objects to drop in a free fall and the acceleration due to gravity is constant, both objects have identical motion.   **7.** No. The value or acceleration due to gravity is 9.8 m/sec/sec. Therefore the distance covered is the same for all objects in free fall in a given time.   **8.** 51.0 kg   **9.** 1 m/sec/sec   **10.** The car would push on the tow truck with a force equal and opposite to the force of the tow truck on the car.

Laboratory Investigation Worksheet: Will an Elephant Fall Faster Than a Mouse?

Observations   1. They will reach the ground at the same time, if air resistance is similar for both.   **2.** Probably, but they may show differences due to inability to drop both items at exactly the same time and from the same height.   **3.** Probably the foam pad, although the paper may reach the ground faster, depending on size and air resistance.   **4.** They should reach the ground at the same time.   **Analysis and**

Conclusions   1. Some observations support the hypothesis, and others do not seem to. When air resistance is made negligible due to the crumpling of paper, however, the hypothesis is shown to be accurate.   **2.** Yes, it did. It reduced air resistance so that the crumpled paper should fall at the same rate as the other objects.   **3.** If air resistance is not an important factor, they will fall at the same rate.   **4.** If mass is the same, the only variable is the shape and size of the object.

Contents

CHAPTER 3 ■ Forces in Fluids

*Appropriate for cooperative learning

© Prentice-Hall, Inc.

Chapter Discovery

Forces in Fluids

Float or Sink

Background Information

Some objects float when placed into a fluid, others sink. What are the characteristics that determine the fate of an object in a fluid? Floating or sinking depends on the mass and volume of the object as well as upon the characteristics of the fluid. In this activity you will discover what happens when an object is placed into a fluid.

Materials

balance scale
cork
small rock
plastic bottle cap
small candle
graduated cylinder
glass-marking pencil

Procedure

1. Use the balance scale to determine the mass of the cork. Record your measurement.

2. Fill half of the graduated cylinder with water. Mark the water level with the marking pencil.

3. Place the cork in the water. Record whether it floats or sinks.

4. Measure the change in the water level by subtracting the original level from the final level. Record the change.

5. Calculate the mass of the displaced water measured in step 4. Every mL of water has a mass of 1 g. Record the mass.

6. Repeat steps 1 through 5 with different objects: rock, bottle cap, and the small candle.

Observations

Data Table

Object	Floats/Sinks	Mass (g)	Volume of Displaced Water	Mass of Displaced Water
cork				
rock				
bottle cap				
candle				

Analysis and Conclusions

1. Which objects floated? Which sank?

_____

_____

2. Look on the table at the data for the objects that floated. What do you notice about the masses of these objects compared with the mass of the water they displaced?

_____

_____

_____

3. Now look at the data for the objects that sank. What do you notice about their masses compared with the mass of the water they displaced?

_____

_____

_____

4. Describe the relationship between the water displaced and whether or not an object sinks or floats.

_____

_____

_____

5. Explain why a large wooden block will float in water, yet a tiny steel bullet will sink.

_____

_____

_____

Activity

Buoyancy and Archimedes' Principle

According to Archimedes' principle, an object placed in a fluid is buoyed up by a force equal to the weight of the displaced fluid.

Sinking Objects

Use the diagram below to provide the missing information.

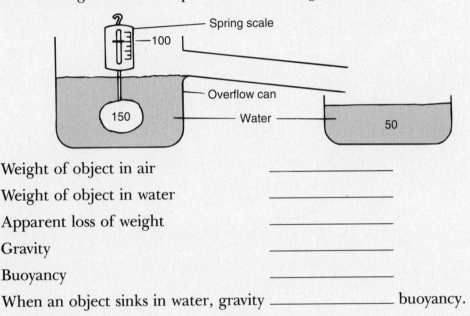

Weight of object in air	_____
Weight of object in water	_____
Apparent loss of weight	_____
Gravity	_____
Buoyancy	_____

When an object sinks in water, gravity _____ buoyancy.

Floating Objects

Use the diagram below to provide the missing information.

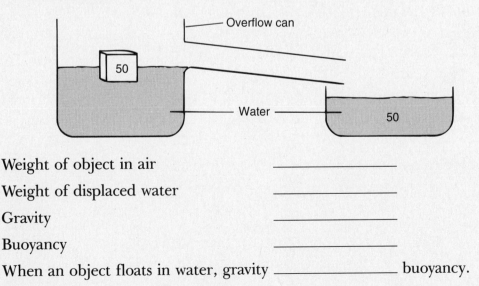

Weight of object in air	_____
Weight of displaced water	_____
Gravity	_____
Buoyancy	_____

When an object floats in water, gravity _____ buoyancy.

ctivity

CHAPTER

3

Pressure in a Liquid

A fluid exerts a pressure in all directions. If an object is placed in a bowl of water, pressure is exerted on all sides of the object. If, however, one side of the object is not in contact with the water, pressure is not equal on all sides. In this activity you will see what happens when the pressure of a liquid is not the same on all sides of a submerged object.

To do this activity you will need the following materials: a hollow tube, such as an orange juice can open at both ends, a metal jar lid, a drinking glass, and a bowl or basin.

Now follow the steps below and learn more about pressure in a liquid.

1. Fill a drinking glass with water.

2. Fill a bowl or basin with water.

3. Place the metal jar lid under the hollow tube. Now, keeping both objects together, place them in the bowl or basin of water. See the accompanying figure for clarification.

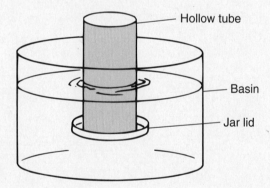

4. Does the jar lid sink to the bottom? _____ Explain your answer. _____

_____

_____

_____

_____

_____

5. Slowly pour water from the drinking glass into the hollow tube. At what point does

the jar lid sink to the bottom? _____

_____

_____

_____

Activity

An Eggciting Experiment

1. Obtain a glass bottle with a neck slightly smaller than the size of an egg.
2. Remove the shell from a hard-boiled egg.
3. Crumple a small piece of paper and place it in the bottle. Carefully light a match and drop it into the bottle. **CAUTION:** *Observe safety rules when using a lighted match.*
4. When the paper catches fire, carefully place the egg in the neck of the bottle. Describe what happens to the egg.

_____
_____
_____

5. The burning paper consumes oxygen in the bottle, causing the pressure inside the bottle to decrease. Explain the behavior of the egg in terms of air pressure.

_____
_____
_____
_____

6. Use the space below to draw a diagram of your experimental setup. Use arrows to indicate the areas of decreased and increased air pressure.

Activity ——————————————————— CHAPTER

Forces in Fluids **3**

Water at Your Fingertip

At some point in your life you have probably been scolded for playing with a drinking straw during a meal—filling it up with your drink and placing your finger over the end so that you could hold the drink in the straw. Actually, without realizing it perhaps, you were experimenting with important properties of pressure.

In this activity you will have an opportunity to try this experiment again.

1. Obtain a glass or other container and a glass rod or drinking straw.
2. Partially fill the glass with water.
3. Place the glass tube or drinking straw into the water.
4. Place your finger over the upper end of the straw and remove it from the water. Note what happens to the water.
5. Raise your finger from the tube. Notice what happens to the water.

   Explain why the water stays in the straw when you lift it up. (Remember atmospheric pressure.)

_____

_____

_____

_____

_____

_____

Explain why the water drops out of the straw when you lift your finger.

_____

_____

_____

_____

_____

_____

_____

Name _____ Class _____ Date _____

ctivity

CHAPTER

Forces in Fluids **3**

Fluid Forces

Solve the following problems. Show all your work. Remember to include the correct units.

1. What is the pressure applied by a piston that has an area of 10 cm² and exerts a force of 10 N?

2. A 0.7-kg mass measures 5 cm in width, 10 cm in length, and 2 cm in height. It is resting on a wooden floor.

   a. What pressure does it exert on the floor?

   b. If it is turned so that the 5-cm and 2-cm sides are in contact with the floor, will the pressure on the floor be increased or decreased?

3. What volume will a gas occupy at 975 mm of pressure if the gas occupies 525 cc at 650 mm of pressure?

4. A container with equal sides of 10 cm is filled with 500 g of fluid.

   a. What is the force in newtons on the bottom of the container?

   b. What is the density of the fluid in grams per cubic centimeter?

   c. What is the pressure on the bottom of the container in newtons per square centimeter?

—————————— *Laboratory Investigation* ——————————

A Cartesian Diver

Problem

What is the relationship between the density of an object and its buoyancy in a fluid?

Materials *(per group)*

copper wire
medicine dropper
large, clear-plastic bottle with an airtight lid
glass
water

Procedure

1. Wrap several turns of wire around the middle of the medicine dropper.

2. Fill the glass with water and place the dropper in the glass. The dropper should barely float, with only the very top of it above the surface of the water.

3. If the dropper floats too high, add more turns of wire. If the dropper sinks, remove some turns of wire.

4. Completely fill the large plastic bottle with water.

5. Place the dropper in the bottle of water. The water should overflow.

6. Screw the cap tightly on the bottle. No water or air should leak out when the bottle is squeezed.

7. Squeeze the sides of the bottle. Record your observations. If the dropper does not move, take it out and add more turns of wire.

8. Release the sides of the bottle. Record your observations.

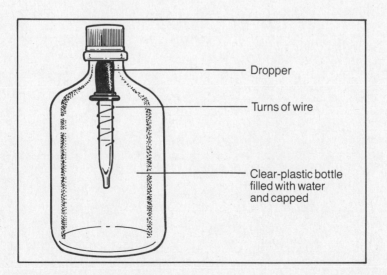

Dropper

Turns of wire

Clear-plastic bottle
filled with water
and capped

Observations

1. What happens to the dropper when the sides of the bottle are squeezed? _____

_____

_____

2. What happens to the dropper when the sides of the bottle are released? _____

_____

_____

Analysis and Conclusions

1. What happens to the pressure of the water when you squeeze the sides of the

bottle? _____

_____

_____

2. When you squeeze the bottle, some of the water is pushed up into the dropper.

Why? _____

_____

_____

3. Why does the dropper sink when you squeeze the sides of the bottle? _____

_____

_____

4. Why does the dropper rise when you release the sides of the bottle? _____

_____

_____

5. How is the density of an object related to its buoyancy in a fluid? _____

_____

_____

6. On Your Own Leave the experimental setup in a place where you can observe it at various times of the day. What does it show about air pressure over a period of several days?

_____

_____

Answer Key

Chapter Discovery: Float or Sink

1. The cork and the bottle cap should float. The rock and the candle should sink. **2.** The mass of the object is less than or equal to the mass of the water it displaced. **3.** The mass of the object is greater than the mass of the water it displaced. **4.** An object floats if it displaces an amount of water with a mass equal to or greater than its own mass. An object sinks when it displaces an amount of water with a mass less than its own mass. **5.** Students should realize that the small amount of water displaced by the bullet does not have enough mass to equal the mass of the steel. The larger amount of water displaced by the wooden block has enough mass to equal or exceed that of the wood.

Activity: Buoyancy and Archimedes' Principle

Sinking Objects 150 100 50 150 50 is greater than
Floating Objects 50 50 50 50 is equal to (or less) than

Discovery Activity: Pressure in a Liquid

4. No. The pressure exerted by the fluid (water) pushing up on the underside of the lid is greater than the pressure pushing down on it. Because there is no water in the hollow tube, there is no water pressure. Water pressure on all sides of the object is not equal because one side is not in contact with the water. **5.** The jar lid sinks to the bottom when the level of water in the hollow tube is equal to the level of water in the bowl or basin.

Discovery Activity: An Eggciting Experiment

The burning paper heated the air in the bottle and caused the air to expand. As it expanded, the air was forced out past the egg, making the egg bounce up and down. When the pressure in the bottle decreased, the pressure of the air pressing down on the egg forced the egg into the bottle.

Activity: Water at Your Fingertip

When you lift the straw you are preventing air pressure from pushing down on the top of the water. Because air pressure is exerted in every direction, air pressure at the bottom of the straw pushes up on the water preventing it from dropping out of the straw. When you raise your finger, the air pressure from above and the weight of the water in the straw are greater than the air pressure from below and the water drops out.

Problem-Solving Activity: Fluid Forces

1. 1 N/cm^2 **2a.** 0.14 N/cm^2 **b.** increased
3. 350 cm^3 **4a.** 4.9 N **b.** 0.5 g/cc
c. 0.049 N/cm^2

Laboratory Investigation Worksheet: A Cartesian Diver

Observations **1.** The dropper sinks. **2.** The dropper rises. **Analysis and Conclusions** **1.** The pressure increases. **2.** By squeezing the bottle, you are applying pressure. This pressure is felt throughout the liquid. The increased pressure forces water into the dropper. **3.** The increased pressure forces water into the dropper, increasing the density of the dropper, so it sinks. **4.** When you release the sides of the bottle, you decrease the pressure, so water comes out of the dropper and the density decreases, so it rises. **5.** The greater the density, the less buoyancy. **6.** The dropper will probably rise and fall slightly over a period of several days. This shows that the air pressure outside the bottle is not constant.

Contents

CHAPTER 4 ■ Work, Power, and Simple Machines

*Appropriate for cooperative learning

Chapter Discovery

Work, Power, and Simple Machines

It's All Uphill

Background Information
When you have a difficult task to do, you often try to find ways to make that task, your work, easier. Whether you find a device specifically designed for that task, or whether you create something yourself, you have somehow decreased the amount of work you must do. There are definite physical reasons why your task is made easier. In this activity you will discover an important relationship that explains why.

Materials
small toy wagon or truck
board about 60 cm × 15 cm
spring scale
several books
string

Procedure
1. Place one end of the board on a pile of three or four books and let the other end rest on the table. Measure the length of the board from the floor to the corner of the top book. Record this measurement.
2. Attach one end of the string to the wagon and the other to the spring scale. Pull the wagon up the board. Record the amount of force required.
3. Raise the pile of books and repeat steps 1 and 2.
4. Lower the pile of books and repeat steps 1 and 2.

Observations

	Distance Up Board (cm)	Force Required (N)
Trial 1		
Trial 2		
Trial 3		

Analysis and Conclusions

1. In which trial did the wagon move the longest distance? Shortest?

   _____

2. Which trial required the greatest force? Least force?

   _____

3. What is the relationship between the force required and the distance moved?

   _____

   _____

4. How could you decrease the required force even further?

   _____

   _____

5. What are some examples of slanted surfaces, or inclines?

   _____

   _____

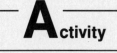

Odd Term Out

In each of the following numbered sets of terms, three of the terms belong together, and one term does not belong. Read each set of terms, decide what characteristic three of them share, and then underline the term that does *not* belong.

1. wedge, pulley, inclined plane, screw

2. sled, barber's chair, rescue ladder, auto lift

3. work input, buoyancy, efficiency, work output

4. mechanical advantage, joule/sec, power, watt

5. ramp, fulcrum, lever, seesaw

6. newton-meter, watt, joule, work

7. shovel, steering wheel, block and tackle, typewriter

8. machine, multiplies force, multiplies work, redirects force

9. greatest efficiency, least friction, most friction, well lubricated

10. density = volume/mass, work = force × distance, power = work/time, efficiency = work output/work input

Activity

Work, Power, and Simple Machines

CHAPTER
4

Types of Levers

Identify the class of each lever shown below.

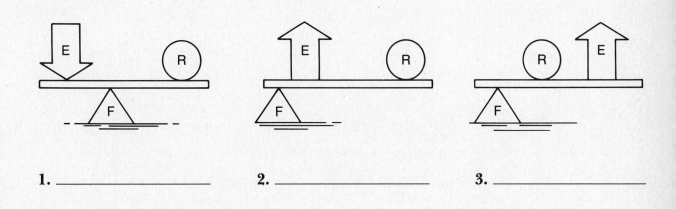

1. _____   2. _____   3. _____

Identify the class of each of the following levers. Then indicate the position of the fulcrum, resistance force, and effort force by using the letters F, R, and E to label each diagram.

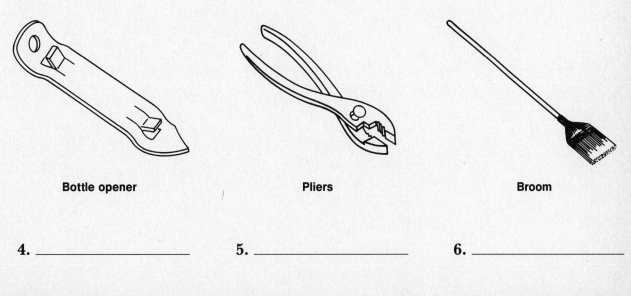

Bottle opener   **Pliers**   **Broom**

4. _____   5. _____   6. _____

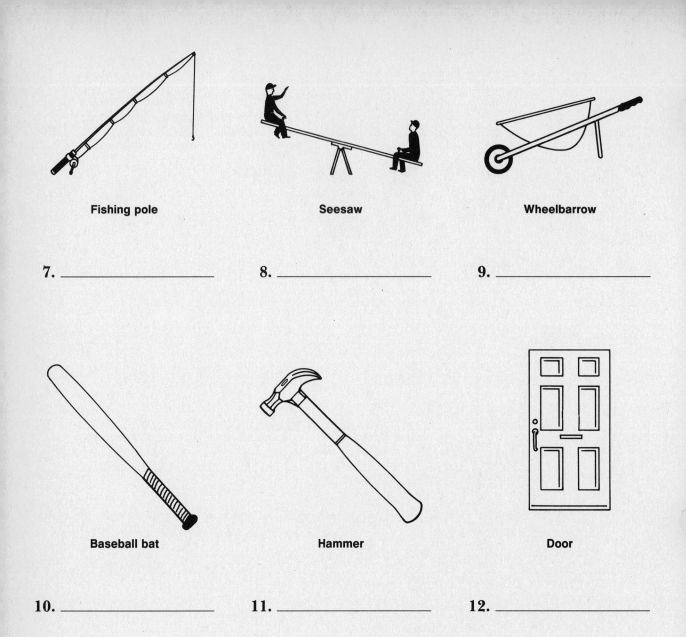

Fishing pole

Seesaw

Wheelbarrow

7. _____

8. _____

9. _____

Baseball bat

Hammer

Door

10. _____

11. _____

12. _____

ctivity

Work and Power

Solve the following problems. Show all your work. Remember to include the correct units.

1. A force of 10,000 N is applied to a stationary wall. How much work is performed?

2. A 950-N skydiver jumps from an altitude of 3000 m. What is the total work performed on the skydiver?

3. A bulldozer performs 80,000 N-m of work pushing dirt a distance of 16 m. What is the force of the dirt?

4. An ant does 1 N-m of work in dragging a 0.0020-N grain of sugar. How far does the ant drag the sugar?

5. You are walking from your math class to your science class. You are carrying books that weigh 20 N. You walk 45 m down the hall, climb 15 m up the stairs, and then walk another 30 m to your science class. What is the total work performed on your books?

6. A horse performs 15,000 J of work pulling a wagon for 20 sec. What is the horse's power?

7. A 750-N pole vaulter lifts himself 5.0 m high in 2.5 sec. What is his power?

8. A pump drains a small pond by performing 120,000 J of work. The power rating of the pump is 1000 w. How long does it take to drain the pond?

9. A tow truck pulls a car out of a ditch in 6.5 seconds. If 6000 w of power is used, how much work is performed by the truck?

10. An elevator lifts five passengers 30 m in 24 sec. The power is 15,000 w. What is the total weight of the elevator and passengers?

Activity Work, Power, and Simple Machines

Calculating Work and Power

Solve the following problems. Show all your work. Remember to include the correct units.

1. How much work is done by a crane that lowers 1000 N of material a distance of 150 m?

2. How much work is done when a 1-kg mass is raised a vertical distance of 1 m?

3. A 5-kg rock is lifted 2 m in 5 sec.

  a. How much work is done?

  b. What power is used?

4. A teacher pushed a 10-kg desk across a floor for a distance of 5 m. She exerted a horizontal force of 20 N. How much work was done?

5. A weight lifter lifts a 150-kg barbell above his head from the floor to a height of 2 m. He holds the barbell there for 5 sec. How much work does he do during that 5-sec interval?

6. A student who weighs 500 N climbed the stairs from the first floor to the third floor, 15 m above, in 20 sec.

   a. How much work did she do?

   b. What was her power?

7. A box is pushed across the floor for a distance of 5 m with a force of 50 N in 5 sec.

   a. How much work is done?

   b. What is the power?

   c. If the box is pushed back again, what is the total amount of work done?

8. A woman lifts a 35-kg child a distance of 1.5 m and carries her forward for 6.5 m.

   a. How much work does the woman do in lifting the child?

   b. How much work does the child do?

9. If 4000 N are used to raise a 30-kg mass, how high is the mass raised?

10. A force used to lift a 12-kg mass to a height of 8 m in 2 sec does 1040 J of work.

   a. How much force is used?

   b. What power is developed?

Laboratory Investigation

CHAPTER 4 ■ Work, Power, and Simple Machines

Up, Up, and Away!

Problem
How do pulleys help you to do work?

Materials *(per group)*
ring stand and ring
spring balance calibrated in newtons
weight
string
single pulley

Procedure
1. Tie one end of a small piece of string around the weight. Tie the other end to the spring balance. Weigh the weight. Record the weight in newtons. Untie the string and weight.
2. Attach the ring about one half to three fourths of the way up the ring stand.
3. To construct a single fixed pulley, hang the pulley directly onto the ring as shown.
4. Tie the weight to one end of a string.
5. Pass the other end of the string over the pulley and tie it to the spring balance.
6. Pull down slowly and steadily on the spring balance and record the force needed to raise the weight.
7. To make a single movable pulley, tie one end of a string to the ring.
8. Pass the other end of the string under the pulley and tie it to the spring balance as shown.
9. Attach the weight directly onto the pulley.
10. Raise the weight by pulling the spring balance upward. Record the force shown on the spring balance.

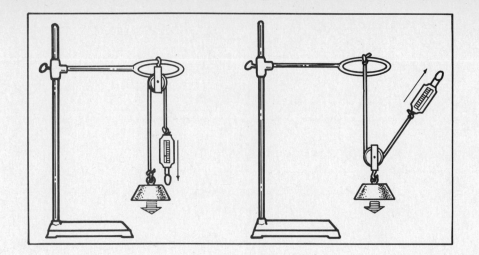

Observations

1. How much force was needed to lift the weight using the fixed pulley? _____

_____

2. How much force was needed to lift the weight using the movable pulley? _____

_____

Analysis and Conclusions

1. How does a fixed pulley help you do work? _____

_____

_____

2. How does a movable pulley help you do work? _____

_____

_____

3. What could you do to lift an object with greater ease than either the fixed pulley or

the movable pulley alone? _____

_____

_____

4. **On Your Own** Using what you learned about pulleys, figure out how many movable

pulleys you would need to lift a 3600-N boat using a force of 450 N? _____

_____

_____

Answer Key

Chapter Discovery: It's All Uphill

1. Trial 3 (least number of books); Trial 2 (greatest number of books)   2. Trial 2; Trial 3.   3. The greatest distance required the least force and the shortest distance required the most force. As distance increases, force decreases and as distance decreases, force increases.   4. To decrease force, you must increase distance.   5. Examples will vary. Check for accuracy. Some ideas are a ramp, a road on a hill, a gang plank, a stairway.

Activity: Odd Term Out

1. pulley   2. sled   3. buoyancy
4. mechanical advantage   5. ramp
6. watt   7. typewriter 8. multiplies work   9. most friction   10. density = volume/mass

Activity: Types of Levers

1. first class   2. third class   3. second class
4. second class   5. first class   6. third class
7. third class   8. first class   9. second class
10. third class   11. first class   12. second class

Problem-Solving Activity: Work and Power

1. 0 N-m   2. 2,850,000 N-m   3. 5000 N-m

4. 500 m   5. 1800 N-m   6. 750 W
7. 1500 W   8. 120 sec   9. 39,000 J
10. 12,000 N

Problem-Solving Activity: Calculating Work and Power

1. 150,000 N-m   2. 9.8 N-m   3a. 98 N-m   b. 19.6 W   4. 100 N-m   5. none
6a. 7500 N   b. 375 W   7a. 250 N-m b. 50 W   c. 500 N-m   8a. 514.5 N-m   b. none
9. 13.6 m   10a. 130 N   b. 520

Laboratory Investigation Worksheet: Up, Up, and Away!

Observations   1. The force needed to lift the weight using the single fixed pulley equals the weight of the weight.   **2.** The force needed to lift the weight using the single movable pulley is one half the weight of the weight.   **Analysis and Conclusions   1.** A fixed pulley changes the direction of the force.   **2.** A movable pulley changes the amount of force needed to lift or move an object.   **3.** Create a pulley system containing both fixed and movable pulleys.   **4.** A mechanical advantage of 8 would be needed to lift the boat because 3600 ÷ 450 = 8. A pulley system similar to the right-hand pulley in Figure S4–22, but with 8 pulleys rather than 6, could be used to lift the boat.

Contents

*Appropriate for cooperative learning

—**C**hapter Discovery

Energy: Forms and Changes

CHAPTER

5

All Steamed Up

Background

Sometimes you are just too tired too move. You might say that you have no energy. Other times, you go nonstop all day. In this case, you may say that you are filled with energy. Although the concept of energy is much more complex and important than this example, it shows you that you are already familiar with the basic concept of energy. Energy is involved any time a change occurs such as moving from one place to another.

Materials

tea kettle
water
hot plate
cork
string (about 40 cm)

Procedure

1. Fill a tea kettle about halfway with water. Place the kettle on a hot plate.
   CAUTION: *Always be careful when working with a heat source.*

2. Tie a string around the cork so the cork hangs freely.

3. Hold the string so that the cork is positioned about 10 cm above the spout of the tea kettle. It should be in line with the path the steam will take when the water in the kettle boils. Hold the cork still.

4. Turn on the heat source with your free hand or have a partner do it.

5. Heat the water in the kettle until it begins to boil and release steam. **CAUTION:** *Do not let your hand get too close to the steam.* Observe what happens to the cork.

6. Turn down the heat and observe what happens to the cork.

Analysis and Conclusions

1. What happened to the cork when the steam hit it?

   _____

   _____

   _____

2. What happened to the cork when the heat was turned down?

_____

_____

_____

3. You observed the basic process behind a steam engine. A steam engine uses steam to move machinery. Can you explain how this might work?

_____

_____

_____

_____

4. Was energy involved in this experiment? How do you know?

_____

_____

_____

5. Energy appears in different forms. Electric energy as in electrical outlets, heat energy as found in hot materials, and chemical energy in the particles that make up a substance are some examples. Was there more than one type of energy in this experiment? If so, what were they?

_____

_____

_____

ctivity

Recognizing Potential and Kinetic Energy

Each labeled item represents a source of either potential energy or kinetic energy or both. Fill in the spaces with the correct word(s).

Name _____ Class _____ Date _____

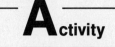
Observing Kinetic Energy and Potential Energy

1. In the appropriate column, write down all the objects that you can observe in 1 minute that have kinetic energy.

2. Repeat step 1 for objects that have potential energy.

Kinetic Energy	Potential Energy

3. Write a conclusion about the relative number of objects that have kinetic energy versus the number that have potential energy.

_____

_____

_____

_____

_____

Name _____ Class _____ Date _____

Activity _____ CHAPTER

Energy: Forms and Changes **5**

Energy

Solve the following problems. Show all your work. Remember to include the correct units.

1. What is the kinetic energy of a 24-kg mass that is moving with a velocity of 2 m/sec?

2. A baseball that weighs 1.38 N is thrown so that it attains a velocity of 18 m/sec. What is the kinetic energy of the ball at that velocity?

3. A 10-kg mass is lifted to a height of 2 m.
   a. What is its weight?

   b. What is its potential energy at that height?

   c. How much work is done in lifting the mass? (Neglect friction.)

4. A rock with a weight of 156.8 N falls 5 m. What potential energy does it have just before the end of its fall?

5. How many joules of energy are produced when 1/1000 kg of mass is changed into energy?

Energy Changes

The diagrams below represent objects in which energy conversions take place. Using the number assigned to each item, complete the table by placing the number in the box that represents the energy conversion for that object. Think of some examples to fill in the blank boxes that remain after you have identified each of the diagrams.

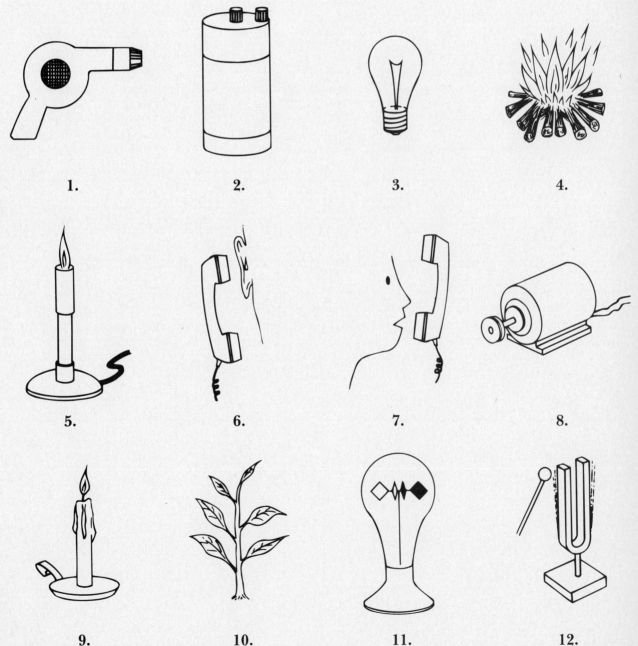

1.   2.   3.   4.

5.   6.   7.   8.

9.   10.   11.   12.

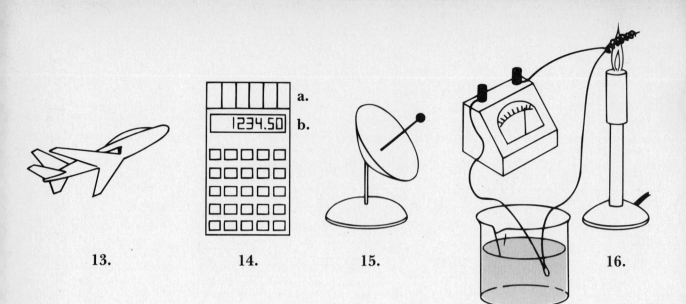

13.

14.
a.
b.

15.

16.

TO	FROM					
	Heat	Light	Sound	Chemical	Mechanical	Electric
Heat						
Light						
Sound						
Chemical						
Mechanical						
Electric						

 ctivity _____

Energy: Forms and Changes

CHAPTER

5

Energy Calculations

1. Does an object have energy when it is at rest? Explain your answer.

    _____

    _____

    _____

2. A 250-kg rock falls off a cliff and comes to rest on the ground, which is 40 m below the cliff. At what point is the rock's potential energy at maximum?

    _____

    Where is the kinetic energy at maximum?

    _____

3. At what height is an object that weighs 490 N if its gravitational potential energy is 4900 N-m?

4. What is the power of a machine that does 1800 N-m of work per minute?

5. A girl on a motorbike passes by at a speed of 15 m/sec. Her mass is 40 kg. What is her kinetic energy?

6. What speed does a 1-kg mass have when its kinetic energy is 1 N-m?

7. How fast is a 6-kg sphere traveling if it has 55 N-m of energy?

8. The constant value for the speed of light (c) is 3×10^8 m/sec. What is the mass equivalent of 100,000 N-m of energy?

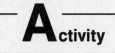ctivity

Energy: Forms and Changes

Automobile Energy

1. Use the accompanying graphs to answer the following questions.

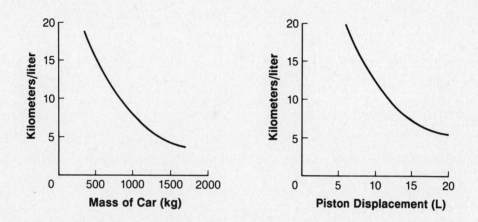

a. What is the effect of piston displacement on fuel economy?

_____

_____

_____

b. To what do you think piston displacement refers?

_____

_____

_____

c. What is the effect of the mass of the car on fuel economy?

_____

_____

_____

d. In what two ways could the fuel economy of a car be increased?

_____

_____

2. Rate the following in terms of energy efficiency, starting with the least efficient.

automobile   walking   train   bicycle   bus   airplane

_____

_____

3. What other factors besides fuel economy should be considered in selecting a car?

_____

_____

Laboratory Investigation

Relating Mass, Velocity, and Kinetic Energy

Problem
How does a change in mass affect the velocity of an object if its kinetic energy is constant?

Materials *(per group)*
rubber band
3 thumbtacks
12 washers glued together in groups of 2, 4, and 6
wooden board, 15 cm × 100 cm
meterstick

Procedure 👁 ▆

1. Place three thumbtacks at one end of the wooden board, as shown in the figure.
2. Stretch the rubber band over the three thumbtacks to form a triangle.
3. In front of the rubber band, place two washers that have been stuck together.
4. Pull the washers and the rubber band back about 2 cm, as in the figure. Release the rubber band. The washers should slide about 70 to 80 cm along the board.
5. Practice step 4 until you can make the double washer travel 70 to 80 cm each time.
6. Mark the point to which you pulled the rubber band back to obtain a distance of 70 to 80 cm. This will be your launching point for the entire experiment.

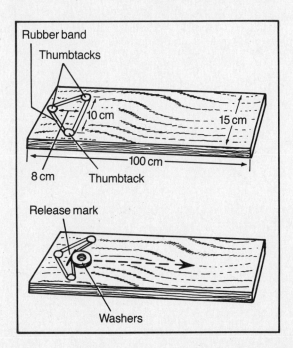

7. Launch the double washer three times. In a data table, record the distance in centimeters for each trial. Remember to use the same launching point each time.

8. Repeat step 7 for a stack of 4 washers.

9. Repeat step 7 for a stack of 6 washers.

Observations

Calculate the average distance traveled by 2 washers, 4 washers, and 6 washers.

_____

Analysis and Conclusions

1. What is the relationship between the mass, or number of washers, and the average

   distance traveled? _____

   _____

   _____

2 What kind of energy was in the washers when you held them at the launching point?

   How do you know? _____

   _____

   _____

3. After the washers were launched, what kind of energy did they have? _____

   _____

   _____

4. You launched all the washers from the same position. Was the energy the same for

   each launch? _____

   _____

   _____

5. Assume that the farther the washers slid, the greater their initial velocity. Did the

   heavier group of washers move faster or slower than the lighter group? _____

   _____

   _____

6. If the kinetic energy is the same for each set of washers, what happens to the

   velocity as the mass increases? _____

   _____

   _____

Answer Key

Chapter Discovery: All Steamed Up

1. The cork should move back and forth vigorously.   **2.** The cork should slow down and eventually stop moving.   **3.** Students should suggest that a steam engine must build up enough steam to move more massive objects than the cork.   **4.** Energy is involved any time something moves. Because the cork moved, energy must have been involved.   **5.** Although students are not yet familiar with detailed descriptions of the different types of energy, they should realize that the electricity from the outlet somehow made the hot plate produce heat, which made the water produce steam which moved the cork. This should help them discover the basic idea of energy.

Activity: Recognizing Potential and Kinetic Energy

Check answers to see that they agree with illustration.

Activity: Observing Kinetic Energy and Potential Energy

Answers will vary. Check to make sure that students have entered their observations in the correct column.

Problem-Solving Activity: Energy

1. 48   **2.** 23 J   **3a.** 98 N   **b.** 196 J   **c.** 196 J   **4.** 784 J   **5.** 9×10^{13} J

Activity: Energy Changes

Answers will vary slightly. Example: **Row 1** blank, 15, ultrasonic cleaner, 5, bicycle

pump, 1   **Row 2** 9, blank, ?, 4, lighting a match, 3   **Row 3** steam whistle, ?, blank, 4, 12, 6   **Row 4** 14a, 10, ?, blank, safety matches, storage battery charging   **Row 5** steam engine, 11, phonograph recording, 13, blank, 8   **Row 6** 16, 14b, 7, 2, generator, blank

Problem-Solving Activity: Energy Calculations

1. Yes. It has potential energy relative to its position.   **2.** at the top of the path, just as the rock begins to fall; at the bottom of the fall, just before the rock hits the ground   **3.** 10 m   **4.** 30 W   **5.** 4500 N-m   **6.** 1.41 m/sec   **7.** 4.3 m/sec   **8.** 1.1×10^{-12}

Discovery Activity: Automobile Energy

1a. The larger the piston displacement, the lower the fuel economy.   **b.** the size of the piston   **c.** The larger the mass of a car, the lower the fuel economy.   **d.** Piston displacement and mass of car should be made smaller.   **2.** airplane, automobile, train, bus, walking, bicycle   **3.** safety, cost, comfort, appearance

Laboratory Investigation Worksheet: Relating Mass, Velocity, and Kinetic Energy

Observations Answers will vary, but students should note that the average distance traveled by the fewest washers will be the greatest.
Analysis and Conclusions   1. The smaller the mass, the greater the distance.
2. Potential energy because they have stored energy provided by you when you move them.   **3.** Kinetic energy, or energy of motion.   **4.** Yes.   **5.** Slower.   **6.** Decreases.

Science Reading Skills

TO THE TEACHER

One of the primary goals of the *Prentice Hall Science* program is to help students acquire skills that will improve their level of achievement in science. Increasing awareness of the thinking processes associated with communicating ideas and reading content materials for maximum understanding are two skills students need in order to handle a more demanding science curriculum. Teaching reading skills to junior high school students at successive grade levels will help ensure the mastery of science objectives. A review of teaching patterns in secondary science courses shows a new emphasis on developing concept skills rather than on accumulating factual information. The material presented in this section of the Activity Book serves as a vehicle for the simultaneous teaching of science reading skills and science content.

The activities in this section are designed to help students develop specific science reading skills. The skills are organized into three general areas: comprehension skills, study skills, and vocabulary skills. The Science Gazette at the end of the textbook provides the content material for learning and practicing these reading skills. Each Science Gazette article has at least one corresponding science reading skill exercise.

Contents

Guion Bluford: *Challenger* in Space
Science Reading Skill: Making Predictions

One of the most important and practical skills that can come from the study of science is the ability to make predictions. There is no mystery about making predictions. You do not need a crystal ball. You probably have had some experience in making predictions. Although you may not realize it, every time you use a "hunch" or make a "guess" about what will happen in a certain situation, you are making a prediction. Reviewing questions that you believe will be on a test or taking an umbrella to school because you think it is going to rain are examples of making predictions.

The method used for prediction involves applying what you already know to a given set of conditions and thinking logically. When you read science material, use the same method. This exercise will help you sharpen your skill in making predictions.

A number of conditions are listed in Column A. In Column B are predictions based on these conditions. Select one condition from Column A that corresponds to each prediction in Column B. Write the numbers of your answers in the proper spaces on the chart.

Column A: Conditions

1. A person follows his or her dream and works very hard.
2. Astronauts practice in simulators but have not yet gone on an actual flight.
3. A person has a strong interest in engineering but is not very interested in school.
4. Scientists study the effects of weightlessness on human beings.
5. Guy is told that he cannot accomplish his goals.

Column B: Predictions

1. He or she does not succeed in entering that field.
2. He or she works even harder to achieve what he or she wants.
3. On his or her first flight, he or she encounters some unexpected conditions.
4. He or she learns how to prevent certain health problems in space.
5. He or she succeeds.

	A. Conditions	B. Predictions
1		
2		
3		
4		
5		

Science Reading Skill: Vocabulary Skills

Having a large vocabulary is a key to understanding what you read. You can expand your vocabulary by determining the meaning of a word, remembering that meaning, and using the word as often as you can. Sometimes the meaning of a word is made clear by the way it is used in a sentence, or by its context.

The following list of words is taken from this article. On the line to the right of each word, write its definition. Then on the line to the left of the word, indicate how you determined its meaning. Use the letter C if you figured out the meaning from the context, K if you already knew the meaning, and D if you had to refer to the dictionary.

_____ **1.** aerospace _____

_____ **2.** analyze _____

_____ **3.** applicants _____

_____ **4.** simulators _____

_____ **5.** designate _____

_____ **6.** environment _____

_____ **7.** stable _____

_____ **8.** jarred _____

_____ **9.** era _____

_____ **10.** stress _____

Now write a sentence of your own for each vocabulary word.

11. aerospace _____

12. analyze _____

13. applicants _____

14. simulators _____

15. designate _____

16. environment _____

17. stable _____

18. jarred _____

19. era _____

20. stress _____

Robots: Do They Signal Automation or Unemployment?
Science Reading Skill: Making Predictions

A number of conditions are listed in Column A. In Column B are predictions based on these conditions. Select one condition from Column A that corresponds to each prediction in Column B. Write the numbers of your answers in the proper spaces on the chart.

Column A: Conditions

1. Robots are becoming more and more common in assembly-line jobs.
2. Robots can make many kinds of mass-produced goods more quickly and cheaply than factory workers can.
3. People have to design and repair the robots.
4. Many workers are opposed to the switch to robots.
5. Assembly-line workers who lose their jobs in one factory may not be able to find or keep jobs in other factories.

Column B: Predictions

1. New jobs will be created.
2. Assembly-line workers will need retraining.
3. Many factories that use robots will be more successful than factories that use people.
4. The switch to robots will not happen quickly or easily.
5. More assembly-line workers will lose their jobs.

A. Conditions	B. Predictions
	1
	2
	3
	4
	5

Science Reading Skill: Vocabulary Skills

Having a large vocabulary is a key to understanding what you read. You can expand your vocabulary by determining the meaning of a word, remembering that meaning, and using the word as often as you can. Sometimes the meaning of a word is made clear by the way it is used in a sentence, or by its context.

The following list of words is taken from this article. On the line to the right of each word, write its definition. Then on the line to the left of the word, indicate how you determined its meaning. Use the letter C if you figured out the meaning from the context, K if you already knew the meaning, and D if you had to refer to the dictionary.

_____ **1.** welds _____

_____ **2.** automated _____

_____ **3.** industrial _____

_____ **4.** hazardous _____

_____ **5.** technology _____

_____ **6.** generated _____

_____ **7.** displaced _____

_____ **8.** productivity _____

_____ **9.** emigrate _____

_____ **10.** implementation _____

Now write sentences of your own for each vocabulary word above.

11. welds _____

12. automated _____

13. industrial _____

14. hazardous _____

15. technology _____

16. generated _____

17. displaced _____

18. productivity _____

19. emigrate _____

20. implementation _____

Name _____ Class _____ Date _____

Hypersonic Planes: Flying Faster Than the Speed of Sound

Science Reading Skill: Remembering What You Have Read

Remembering is a very important part of learning. To help you remember what you have read, follow these suggestions. Read the title and subtitle. Watch for words in italics or boldfaced print that call your attention to important facts and ideas. Look at the photos and drawings and their captions. Relate the information you have read to anything you may already know about the subject or to any past experiences you may have had. Try to form a mental picture of what is being discussed or described.

How Well Do You Remember?

The following information has been taken from the article you just read. Certain facts have been left out. You are to complete the sentences by supplying the correct information.

1. Sandy and her mother were on their way to the airport to pick up _____

   _____.

2. "But just 100 years ago, you couldn't fly from New York to San Francisco in less

   than _____."

3. "An SST, like the one they used to call the *Concorde,* could cross the Atlantic Ocean

   in _____."

4. "When a plane nears the speed of sound, _____

   _____."

5. "So SST flights were prohibited over _____."

6. "Hypersonic speed is any speed greater than _____

   _____."

Science Reading Skill: Summarizing

Summarizing is the technique of condensing material into a short form. When you study science, summarizing can be a most helpful skill for making notes, reviewing facts, and recalling the subject matter.

Write a summary of the article you just read. Be sure to include all the main ideas. Do not include minor details. Use the lines provided below.

_____

_____

_____

_____

_____

_____

_____

_____

_____

_____

_____

Answer Key

Adventures in Science

Predictions 5, 3, 1, 4, 2 **Vocabulary**
1. concerned with space and the Earth's atmosphere **2.** examine in detail **3.** people who request a position **4.** machines that imitate desired conditions **5.** give a special name or grouping to **6.** surrounding conditions **7.** fixed, not easily moved **8.** shaken from sudden impact **9.** period of time measured from an important event **10.** emphasize **11–20.** Check student sentences for accuracy.

Issues in Science

Conditions 3, 5, 2, 4, 1 **Vocabulary** **1.** fuses metal by using heat **2.** using self-operated machinery **3.** having to do with manufacturing **4.** dangerous **5.** applied science **6.** created **7.** put out of place or job **8.** efficiency of output **9.** leave the country **10.** use **11–20.** Sentences will vary.

Futures in Science

1. Sandy's sister, Maria **2.** five hours **3.** four hours **4.** air bunches up in front of it **5.** the United States **6.** five times the speed of sound **Summarizing** Student answers will vary.